William N. Clarke

What Shall we Think of Christianity?

The Levering lectures before the Johns Hopkins University, 1899

William N. Clarke

What Shall we Think of Christianity?

The Levering lectures before the Johns Hopkins University, 1899

ISBN/EAN: 9783337262570

Printed in Europe, USA, Canada, Australia, Japan

Cover: Foto ©Lupo / pixelio.de

More available books at **www.hansebooks.com**

WHAT SHALL WE THINK
OF CHRISTIANITY?

WHAT SHALL WE THINK OF CHRISTIANITY?

*THE LEVERING LECTURES BEFORE THE
JOHNS HOPKINS UNIVERSITY*

1899

By WILLIAM NEWTON CLARKE, D.D.
Author of
"AN OUTLINE OF CHRISTIAN THEOLOGY."

CHARLES SCRIBNER'S SONS
NEW YORK 1899

THIRD EDITION.

University Press:
JOHN WILSON AND SON, CAMBRIDGE, U.S.A.

These Lectures,

NOW PUBLISHED AS THEY WERE DELIVERED,

ARE DEDICATED, IN GRATEFUL REMEMBRANCE,

TO

MR. EUGENE LEVERING,

The Founder of the Course,

AND

TO THE DELIGHTFUL AUDIENCES THAT LISTENED TO THEM.

CONTENTS.

	PAGE
I. THE CHRISTIAN PEOPLE	1
II. THE CHRISTIAN DOCTRINE	48
III. THE CHRISTIAN POWER	98

The sower went forth to sow his seed: and as he sowed, some fell by the way side; and it was trodden under foot, and the birds of the heaven devoured it. And other fell on the rock; and as soon as it grew, it withered away, because it had no moisture. And other fell amidst the thorns; and the thorns grew with it, and choked it. And other fell into the good ground, and grew, and brought forth fruit a hundredfold. He that hath ears to hear, let him hear.

So is the kingdom of God, as if a man should cast seed upon the earth; and should sleep and rise night and day, and the seed should spring up and grow, he knoweth not how. The earth beareth fruit of herself; first the blade, then the ear, then the full corn in the ear.

WHAT SHALL WE THINK OF CHRISTIANITY?

I

THE CHRISTIAN PEOPLE

I AM heartily glad to speak, in this presence, of the things that occupy my thoughts and make my life, and to speak with the utmost freedom. I shall be glad if what I may say fulfils in some degree the apologetic purpose of this lectureship, by making some Christian realities in which I believe more clear and more helpful to some who listen. I believe in the greatness and worth of Jesus Christ, and I have some sense of the preciousness of his gifts to mankind: and I propose that in these three lectures we look together at three great contributions that he has made to the moral wealth and welfare of humanity. These contributions are the Christian People, the Christian Doctrine, and the Christian Power.

My reason for selecting these three gifts of Christ for consideration is, that these three go far toward making up that great fact in history and life which we call Christianity. When Jesus, the founder of Christianity, left the world, what did he leave behind him that he did not find here? What elements had he added to the life of mankind, and brought in as his contribution to the future? He left in the world, at least in vigorous and promising beginnings, a people, a doctrine, and a power: — a people, few but attentive and receptive; a doctrine, growing into fulness and vitality through their experience; and a power, already operative and of boundless potency. These combined bequests of his had at first no common name. At first their unity could not be clearly discerned. Nevertheless, he had left a unity in the world, not a mere sprinkling of detached results, and in due time the unity asserted itself. After a little his disciples were named, and probably nicknamed, Christians. The nickname stayed upon them, and came to be their chosen name for whatsoever belonged to them in relation to their Master. In the name they gloried, for it denoted that new something, unlike the possessions of mankind, yet normal and suitable to man, which Jesus had brought in. Their church was soon the Christian church, and their doctrine the Christian doctrine; and the unified result of Jesus' presence among men came by and by to be known as Christianity. Both the name and the fact have continued until now. If we seek to know what Christianity is, and of what elements it is composed, how can we describe it better than by saying that it is made up of these three elements, the people, the doctrine, and the power that Jesus left in the world as his abiding gift to man? If we find more than these, we shall find it, I judge, mainly by unfolding what these contain. In every age these three constitute, or at least efficiently represent, what we call Christianity. By means of these the Christian name has been kept alive among men, and the Christian influence has been exerted.

I wish to inquire how well these gifts of Christ, these elements of Christianity, have done their work, and of how much attention they are really worthy now, after so long a time. They all stand for the holy and beneficent name of Jesus, and are supposed to convey to us, each in its own manner, the gift and influence that he brought. All ought to bear a decided apologetic value. Such a value they are universally expected to show. It is assumed that the Christian people fairly represent the human fruit that the Saviour of men intended to produce, that the Christian doctrine fairly expresses what the Master meant to teach, and that the Christian power is such as the Lord of men is satisfied to be exerting. These gifts of Christ are such that in the light of them Christ himself can scarcely fail to be judged. Of this we cannot complain, nor can we imagine that he himself would make objection. He who said of men, "By their fruits ye shall know them," will not refuse to submit to a fair use of the test that he has proposed for others. Christianity may reasonably be estimated in view of these its constituent elements, if only we can manage to do the judging fairly.

Yet how various the judgments are! and we cannot wonder. Some say that the Christian enterprise is the one successful thing in all the world: the people are the salt of the earth, the doctrine is the light of the world, and the power is God's own power for salvation. Others say that these fruits are no special credit to him whose name they bear: long time and little done, poor fruit and little of it, all sorts of imperfections in the people, inconsistencies and irrationalities infesting the doctrine, great unevenness in the operation of the power. All the way between these two extremes the judgments range. We are living now in an atmosphere that is rife with criticism: for there are many who sincerely think that Christianity has been tried in the balances and found wanting, and is justly condemned by its failure to produce a people, a doctrine, or a power proportioned in excellence to its claims.

In what I may have the honor to say in this presence, I desire to show, if possible, what is true about these three gifts of Christ which constitute our Christianity. I wish to look at them fairly, if I can. I am not here to defend what bears the name of Christian merely because it bears that name, nor am I here to surrender what is precious because it is not perfect. I shall inquire what can reasonably be expected of these gifts in the world, and how well they are fulfilling rational expectations. I shall note some of the conditions attendant upon the rise, growth, and continuance of these three elements of Christianity, in order that we may judge, with some fairness, how well they have done their work and realized the aims of Christ. Thus I shall try to ascertain what we ought to think of Christianity. And perhaps we may discern something of the winning and convincing beauty of the Lord in these his gifts.

In the present hour we consider the Christian People.

There is no mystery about the beginning of the Christian people. Jesus left in the world the little band of believers in himself that had gathered around him in his ministry. They were disciples learning of him, and some of them were already named apostles, messengers, or heralds. We read of a hundred and twenty in Jerusalem, and above five hundred, perhaps in Galilee. Very soon the hundreds became thousands. Out from Palestine his name went to the Roman world, and in Antioch, Asia Minor, Greece, and Rome itself, multitudes were added to the Christian company. By the time that Jesus, if he had lived, would have attained to the age of three-score years and ten, the Roman empire was dotted over with Christian churches, and a people devoted to his Name was everywhere.

Who were they, and what? What principles were operative in the formation of the Christian people? How came it to be what it was? I shall be glad if I can set forth and illustrate the simple and commonplace fact that the normal and necessary laws of life had their way here. Christianity, placed in the world, experienced the inevitable, and took the consequences of existence. The Christian people, first and later, was such as it could be.

The Founder, as we know, drew his first followers from among the Jews. Not from the circle of the high religionists did they come, but from that better circle which was found among the common people. Here were the Jewish homes, where religion was pure and sweet, and faith took hold upon the God of the fathers, — where response to a new and holy influence, therefore, was most possible. Out of the common class, the fishermen and the poor, came the first to follow Jesus. Legalism had not blinded the eyes of these to spiritual beauty, and the simple saw the glory of God in the face of Jesus Christ. Ignorant of many things they were, and in religion itself they needed long and patient teaching, yet these were the men and women to whom the Master could say, "Blessed are your eyes for they see, and your ears for they hear."

When the Master had gone, these were his heralds. Enlightened they were in heart by the power of love and the insight that comes from spiritual fellowship, glowing and enthusiastic was their faith, and yet they were themselves, and could proclaim only what had become real to them. No one learns great things thoroughly in a single lesson. It is vain to imagine that the first disciples could know their Master perfectly at once, for even the divine Spirit cannot dispense with the element of time in guiding human beings into truth. The fact simply is that a new, glorious, uplifting, character-making power was taking hold of men. Forth from Jesus came a mighty transforming influence. It took men as it found them, for it could not do otherwise, and it wrought upon them as they could be wrought upon, for it could not do more. It was a heavenly gift amid earthly elements, a divine power working upon human materials. The first Christian people were the human materials upon which this divine power had done, and was doing, its initial work. They were this, and nothing more.

We can trace the process. The Christian message met its inevitable fate in the hearing that it received. The hearers heard with their own ears, and understood by means of their own preconceptions. Every growing thing grows according to the soil that it falls into, and the seed of the word was no exception. In Jerusalem, the message was taken into minds full of inherited Jewish ideas. The better spirit of the Jewish religion and the narrow constraints of Jewish thought conspired to make a Jewish-Christian people, in whom the large conceptions and spiritual aspirations of Jesus could find but scanty welcome. We know how near the new faith came to being smothered to death in a Christian Judaism, and how Paul was the chosen vessel of Christ to carry his name out from these limitations to the Gentiles, the nations of the world. The first group of the Christian people came near burying the gospel alive under their old ideas of narrow religion.

Paul and his companions did carry the Name abroad, and the Name went abroad with power. Through the Roman world it went, everywhere finding its welcome. Multitudes received it with joy, and found fresh life in Christ. Who were these? These too were the poor and untrained. Many of them were slaves, and many others were of low station and narrow life. Christ made life a new and larger thing, and they felt, as they well might feel, that the best thing in the world had come to them. Among the believers were some of large intelligence and power. Some of them could receive the new gift not only into good and honest hearts, but into lives somewhat prepared to bring forth the worthiest fruit. Yet where was the mind wherein there were no conceptions that could enter into union with the new faith only to injure it and diminish its effectiveness? If Jewish legalism, monotheistic though narrow, required time to be outgrown, how must it be with polytheism, with the popular superstitions that hung about immemorial beliefs, and with the moral corruptions that had sprung from the coarse worships of an earlier day? How long would such influences as these linger when a new moral force, still new indeed, was entering to transform the life? Paul rebukes his converts in Corinth for low standards of living, and low vices inherited from a long antiquity, and this is exactly what we might expect. Nothing else was possible than that such evils should abide to trouble the friends of

Christlike goodness in the church. Errors in thought also, misconceptions of the gospel, sprang up from the remains of old thinking. At what date such evils could reasonably be expected to disappear, let him tell who dares to think he knows. A Christian people could not be made except from people who were filled with material of thought and character quite contrary to the aim of Christianity.

Nevertheless the new faith made its people. It was not defeated, it was honorably successful. It was far from making a people that fulfilled its ideal, but it made a people worthy of its endeavor. In the first age there was a distinctively Christian life, lived by a distinctively Christian company of men and women. It was a very simple life, lived by a very simple people, but it was animated in great measure by the holy and gracious mind of Christ. How often have we wished that the glimpses into it that are possible to us were not so very few! Why, we have asked, has not more been preserved to us of the plain common life of the Christians of the first and second centuries? But it is not surprising. They were not a literary folk. Their writers were few, and that they were making history they had no idea. Such glimpses as we do obtain are extremely precious. It was a great gift when we recovered the long-lost "Teaching of the Twelve Apostles," with its simple and unconscious revelation of the people and their ways. Just when and where its scenes were enacted we may not know, but it is certain that here we have a genuine view of life as it was among the early Christians. As we read we see that the life was simple, it was devout, it was brotherly, it was hopeful, it was pure in aim and aspiration. It is easy to paint the Roman life of the first century in black, ignoring the brighter and worthier elements in the common world of that time; and yet, though we paint ever so fairly, it is plain when we view this simple picture of Christian living that a new uplifting force has entered to the great Roman world, and a little group of humanity, if no more, has been introduced to sweeter, purer, worthier life. The limitations of the new people are written into the record as clearly as their virtues, and the common faults of human nature crop out in the conditions that call for counsel and reproof; yet here is a genuine fruit of the presence of Jesus in the world for which our human race may well be thankful.

Still we turn from the picture, and from all companion-pictures that we possess, feeling that the Christians of the first and second centuries, taken as a mass, were not capable of propagating the Christianity that the Founder meant for mankind. They possessed it only in part, and how could they pass on the traditions of a better faith than they held? The inevitable had happened: the new faith had taken such people as it found, and they had received it as they could. But a second inevitable followed. The people were changed by the new faith, but the new faith was changed by the people. Christianity transformed the people toward its likeness, and was in turn transformed by them toward their likeness. Shakespeare, complaining, in one of his Sonnets says,

> "My nature is subdued
> To what it works in, like the dyer's hand."

In the same strain Christianity might speak. It made a new people, better than it found them; but they in turn inevitably made a new Christianity, with its strong points illustrated and confirmed in their experience, but with weakness brought in from their defects. The power of the new faith to produce a people worthy of its aims was inevitably diminished, less or more, by the faults that it was compelled to take into itself from the people through whom it wrought. Intractableness of material modified the force.

Or, in other words, the Christian people, with all its good and evil, with all its strength and weakness, with all its glory and shame, is the true resultant of the force that has been working and the material that it has wrought upon. This is one, out of many, of the historical illustrations of the Master's parable of the four kinds of soil. The good seed of the kingdom was sown in the world, and prospered in its growth according to the soil into which it fell. In some places it took no root at all, and in others it secured only a temporary life. Where it did grow, it sometimes had to grow in soil where there were thorn-roots already in the ground, and it must needs grow up among them. If it is asked why an ideal Christian people did not grow up, sufficient to vanquish all doubts of the transforming power, the answer is that the good seed did not always fall into the clear soil, but often, nay always, into places where there was something to check and something to modify its growth. The good seed is seed in a thorn-field. But then, lest we be discouraged, we may remember that it was in order to redeem the field from the thorns that the seed of Christ was sown, and that in God's world good seed roots deeper, in the long season, than the thorns.

This glance into the early period is enough to illustrate the conditions that insured to the rising Christian people both strength and weakness, victory and disappointment. Similar conditions have always existed. There is no time for detailed description of that which the Christian seed has produced in the thorn-field, but we will glance down the long line of results in history, and see, so far as we may, what manner of people it is that Christ has brought into the world through the Christian grace working amid obstructing influences.

The Christian people has a certain unity; but in what does it consist? There is no one type of humanity, no one nationality or race or class or training represented here. The Christian people is gathered out of all nations and kindreds and peoples and tongues, and yet it is marked by one type of experience and character. Only very broadly can this be asserted, I know, but broadly it can be asserted. There is a set of conceptions and experiences by which the Christian character is dominated, and where these are not, there are no Christians. They did not all come into the world with Christ, but they all gather themselves about him into a character-giving unity. The seriousness of life, the holiness and love of the one God, the reality of sin, free salvation from sin by the divine grace in Christ, human duty learned from God in Christ, an inward power for goodness, a deathless hope, — these are the fundamental conceptions of Christianity, and the Christian people are those whose experience corresponds to these conceptions. Or, more truly, Christ presents these as realities, and the Christian people are those who experience these realities. Such experiences create a type of character. No other religion ever had such experiences to offer, and therefore none ever made a people like the Christian people. Knowledge of God is common enough, but not such knowledge of God: knowledge of sin is common, but not of such deliverance from sin : knowledge of duty, but not such inspiration for duty: hope, but not such hope. When there comes to be a people formed, however imfectly, upon the experience of these realities, that people is the work of Christ.

Members of such a people, bearing such

a character, have been known in all the Christian ages. They have been imperfect, all, with every style and combination of imperfections. Every side of the characteristic experience has been lacking somewhere, and somewhere exaggerated or distorted. They have not understood one another very well, and have often failed to recognize one another. Nevertheless the common quality has marked them, less or more, and they have been brothers whether they knew it or not. The people who know by experience about sin and salvation, and learn their duty from their Saviour God, and lift their eyes to immortality in him, these do make one family, a noble family, and God is not ashamed of them, to be called their God.

A character-making force working upon various and imperfect men will, of course, produce some best results. Some men are best prepared beforehand for Christ's influence, and in some the oppositions are most effectively conquered. These are the leaders, the best fruits. Every religion has its saints, and Christianity has its long calendar and its innumerable saints unnamed. The overtowering souls that stand high above the rest, the ones in whom Christianity has done most, — a noble company they form. If we could clearly behold a group of the great Christians of the world, discerning their real spiritual beauty, we should reverently bear witness to the excellence of the heavenly gift. In the group of greatest Christians we should find men and women of deep and serious heart; persons not light-minded, but to whom life is full of meaning; who know evil, both in themselves and in the world, with a dreadful sense of its reality; who have discerned the infinite grace that freely saves, and come to know the eternal goodness in the God who loves forever; who know the gladness of deliverance from evil, the brightness of hope and the exhilaration of strong endeavor; who have loved their fellows with a divine affection and labored for their good; who know the eagerness of high aims, and have used high powers for highest purposes; and from whom there has gone forth a warm radiance of blessing as they have walked among men. Children of faith, they have endured as seeing him who is invisible. Children of hope, they have purified themselves, even as he is pure. Children of love, they have gazed upon God's glory and been changed into the same image. Mark all their imperfections, not denying a single genuine one, and yet we must bear testimony that these great Christian souls that have been among us are a worthy product of the presence and work of Christ in the world. Without them, how much poorer would the history of our race have been! What would it be to drop from the record the names, and from the human stock the personalities, of Paul and John, of Origen and Athanasius, of Ambrose and Augustine and Monica, of Chrysostom and Gregory the Great and Thomas Aquinas, of Tauler and Thomas à Kempis, of Savonarola and Dante and Michelangelo, of Francis of Assisi and Xavier and Loyola, of Wyclif and Huss, of Luther and Melanchthon, of William the Silent and Cromwell and Gustavus Adolphus, of Baxter and Bunyan, of Milton and George Fox, of Calvin and John Knox, of the Wesleys and Whitefield and Edwards, of Shaftesbury and Gladstone and Leo Thirteenth, of Elizabeth Fry and Florence Nightingale, of Livingstone, Channing, Moody, and Phillips Brooks? If besides these there have stood forth leaders who misrepresented the Christian quality, — which not one even of these has perfectly expressed, — what else can be expected when a holy power is working through imperfect men, whose training has prepared them only in part for their honorable mission?

We must not think that the list of the great adequately represents the Christian people. We must remember the rank and file if we wish to think justly of the whole. Saints are of many kinds, not all equally eminent in the sight of the world. The lesser ones are precious, as well as the greater. Two classes of saints have attracted special admiration. The church has often admired the saints of the cloister, withdrawn from the world, given to meditation and prayer, rebuking the evil of the common life by retirement and reflection upon better things. Eyes that have not been attracted to these have been drawn to the saints of the open field, strong workmen or warriors of the Lord, doing large work and known of all men. But Christ, who gave some as apostles and some as prophets, has also raised up saints of the household, who are mediators of grace and strength to those whom they love; saints of the sick-chamber, who suffer and are strong through the holy faith; saints of the market-place and the workshop, who do the world's common work in the spirit of fidelity and power; citizen-saints, who bless the organized life of man by wise counsel and unselfish living; scholar-saints, who minister knowledge to mankind; and saints of the life of charity, who bear the heart of Christ to the needy. These all fall short of the Lord's ideal, but yet we all know that in them Christ has honorably accomplished his purpose to make for himself a people for his own possession, zealous of good works, powerful for blessing.

Large perversions in the life and practice of the Christian people have of course appeared: what would you look for? We will glance at a classical instance, and see how naturally they came. For a while Christianity was the religion of the martyrs. Pure, simple, and courageous in its common life, it condemned the evil world and insured for itself an honorable hatred. Unswerving in loyalty to the only God, it angered the Roman power again and again, and secured the crown of martyrdom. Martyrdom does not prove a cause to be right, and yet it always carries a strong suggestion to that effect. The church of the martyrs was kept sweet by its trials and perils, and the suffering church was a singing church, joyful in its pains and influential through its fortitude. There is a fine charm about the humble and hopeful church of the catacombs. But the church came out of the catacombs, and was soon placed at the head of the world's affairs. When Constantine professed the Christian name, the name instantly became fashionable. Profession of Christianity was now the way to promotion and advantage: therefore the church-doors were crowded with people rushing in. The so-called Christian people of the middle of the fourth century were most of them not Christians at all, in any worthy sense : they were nominal converts, scarcely changed from the paganism of antiquity. Yet they were the recognized Christian people of the time, and it was inevitable that they should set the key for the Christianity of the time that followed. It is no wonder that the religious life ran low, and the virtue of the gospel partly vanished away from those who bore the holy name. Here was the inevitable again. Victory came naturally, and deservedly, to the fresh and vigorous faith, as against the decaying paganism, but victory brought corruption in its train, from the necessities of the case. The holy power had been thrown out into the field of the world, and for the time, in certain respects, its nature was subdued to what it wrought in, like the dyer's hand.

Another perversion in the common life

of the Christian people, — at least it seems a perversion to us of the nineteenth century, with our irrepressible enterprise and our readiness for risks and conflicts, — came as naturally as this. There came a time when a large part of the best of the Christian people, the most high-minded and the best adapted to useful living, were moved to withdraw from the common life of man. The monastic impulse came, and would not be refused. The souls that were most needed for the universal strife left the field for the life of quietness, and the best leaven for improvement of the evil world was withdrawn into cloisters. Multitudes of the men who would have made the best fathers, and of the women who would have made the best mothers, declined to make contribution to the stock of humanity. The quiet, meditative, non-productive life, withdrawn from the responsibilities to which mankind is born, was held out as holier than the common life, and the monastic ideal was set up for universal admiration. Good results followed, and also evil: great good and great evil. The more largely human we grow, the greater seems the pity that the movement went so far. Yet how inevitably it came about. Face to face stood the good and the evil, the good of the gospel and the evil of the world, the good of the reforming power and the evil, ancient and strong, that ought to be put away. The Christian people had no long traditions of holy warfare to inherit, and had not very well learned the lesson of confidence in the good for which they were set to contend. To many of them the case seemed hopeless: so great a world, how could its evil be conquered? Would it not corrupt even those who tried to bless it? All that they could do was to flee, and hide themselves, and seek the safety of their souls, and pray to God for the victory which they lacked courage to seek in strife. We cannot wonder at the feeling. We can call the motive inferior to the best, as surely it was, but we cannot be surprised at the force of it, or affirm that it was altogether an unworthy motive. It was a pure motive, even if it was not the loftiest. The great secession from the daily working force of Christianity was one of the inevitable incidents in the great warfare.

We cannot now illustrate the process farther. But thus, through the successive periods, the Christian people has gone on, responding to surrounding influences as well as to inward monitions, changing with changing conditions, growing with the common growth of mankind, influenced by the world which it was influencing, and yet maintaining a special quality and value of its own. Very largely it was what it had to be: it had the virtues of its inner grace, and the faults of its inheritance and its surroundings. It could not have been otherwise.

What is the outcome? This is the question that concerns us now. What has the Lord of Christianity to show after all this time? How well does the present Christian people commend the power that came into the world with Christ? How are Christians doing their work as a gift of Christ to humanity? All sorts of opinions are held. Some say that Christian people are demonstrably the salt of the earth, without which very little that is sweet or good would be found among men: and others are sure that whatever power they may once have had is now departed. What shall we say?

The mixed quality of the present outcome calls for no apology. Absolutely, there could be nothing else. Those who discuss the Christian people as if they could expect to find in them an adequate illustration of the ideal of Christ, simply do not know what they are talking about. In the conditions that have surrounded Christianity, such a thing is impossible. So the present Christian people are not to be defended as satisfactory, or condemned as worthless. They are not to be counted upon for perfection, or rejected for imperfection. A resultant necessarily partakes in the nature and quality of all the forces that have produced it. Good and evil, strength and weakness, are certain to be present here. Christianity is the life of God in the soul of man, and its human outcome must partake in the qualities both of God and of man.

If we inquire about the Christian people of the present day, they must be estimated in view of an element that I have not yet mentioned. I mean the great transition, the tremendous revolution, of our time. It is not as if the Christian people had attained to a platform where they could be exhibited. On the contrary, they are passing through the severest transition, perhaps, in all their history.

Into this transition more elements enter than I can now name. Our part of the human race is at last beginning to possess a real self-consciousness. Information, in inconceivably vast amount, is being thrown upon the thought of the time, to be handled and assimilated. Thought is passing over from the old non-scientific methods to the more nearly scientific movement that modern study has developed. Facts are scrutinized with new zeal, and truth is tested in new ways. Inquiry knows no bounds. Antiquity and prescription count for nothing. We desire to know the very thing that is, and our certainties are differently grounded from those that our fathers held. Vast social problems arise, in which we are compelled to find out whether we are living together as we ought, and what we owe to one another. All fields of thought are transformed, and all modes and significances of life are altered, in this great time of change. Every period is a period of transition, but there has never been one like this.

Amid these great changes the Christian people, as I conceive, have three things to do. Three things are required of them by the nature of the Christianity which they represent, and in these they must not be found wanting. The Christian people are called to-day to hold their faith, to open their minds, and to expand their hearts. First, to hold their faith. They are called to hold fast their sense of spiritual reality; not to be shaken from their confidence in that living God whom they and their fathers have known; to cling to the reality of religious life and the presence of divine help; to be religious in tenderness of spirit and heavenliness of mind, when the age is almost forgetting to be religious. Next, to open their minds. They are called to perceive that they are living in a new age; to believe in the validity of all facts and be willing to go where facts may lead; to accept reconstructions; to let knowledge in, well assured that it will not drive faith out; to be as free with knowledge as they are with faith. And while these two works go on, the Christian people are called also to expand their hearts, so that they shall be loving men with Christ's own love; to rejoice with them that rejoice and weep with them that weep and plan for them that suffer; to bear the burdens of humanity with wise and helpful tenderness; to forswear aristocratic exclusiveness and minister to men as men, as Jesus did. This great threefold calling is the present calling of the Christian people.

How are they fulfilling it? Not altogether well, or altogether ill. It is the inevitable again. We have to confess that there is much division of labor here: some hold their faith while others open their minds: some open their minds while others expand their hearts. This is not strange, for in a great mass of people it is only natural that one part of the general duty should be more worthily done by some than by others. A certain distribution of parts cannot fail to occur. Yet this is not the ideal. It is to be desired that every one of the Christian people should hold his faith, open his mind, and expand his heart. And toward the ideal there is some progress. Far from perfectly, yet more and more, it is coming to pass. The Christian people respond but slowly to demands upon them, — so slowly that it is easy to be impatient with them, — and yet they do respond. The mind does open, and yet the faith is held, and meanwhile the heart expands in love and helpfulness. Imperfectly and slowly, yet really, the Christian people are at least beginning to rise to the demands of the present age.

It would be pleasant to praise the Christian people here, to point out their better works and tell how well they are doing. But instead of this I shall do what perhaps my auditors do not expect of me. I believe that the danger that the Christian people may miss their calling is greater than the need of praise for their successes: and a few words in this strain I must speak. I greatly fear that many among them may fail to hold their faith. I fear that many may fail to open their minds. I fear that many may fail to expand their hearts. And my anxiety gives me a message.

By failing to hold their faith I do not mean failing to keep their opinions. By faith I mean something more precious far: I mean the living sense of unseen spiritual realities, and firm trust in the living God. What I fear is that many Christians may not "see him who is invisible," and not live in the presence of the Father who is in secret. The danger is that they may be content with holding opinions and mistaking them for faith, and be without that undying sense of reality in God to which alone the noble name of faith belongs. They will then preach unreally, and talk insincerely, and live feebly. They will be Christians in name, but the secret of power will be theirs no longer. And I fear no less that many Christians may fail to open their minds. I know the difficulty, only too well. The very effort to hold their faith may lead them to keep their minds closed against knowledge that no honest mind can permanently refuse. To open the mind and hold the inner sense of spiritual reality is not easy for all. There are men enough who tell us that it cannot be done, and will not long be attempted. Unbelievers in Christianity declare the impossibility from one side, and a large class of Christians from the other. I am afraid that too many of the Christian people, mistaught from both sides, may come to be convinced, and hold their minds unworthily closed. When I reflect upon the profoundly conservative instincts of religious tradition, and the surprising and revolutionary quality of much of the truth that our time brings freshly forth to us, I fear greatly that the impulse of resistance may be too strong for hosts of minds that ought to be opening themselves to present truth in faith upon the present God, and the victory may be where it ought not. And yet again I fear that the Christian people may fail to expand their hearts in helpful and sympathetic love to the men around them. I think I fear this most of all. I know how strong is the temptation to make love an abstract virtue, and consider it sufficient to love God whom we have not seen, while the brother whom we have seen makes no appeal to us. I know how powerful the aristocratic connections of much of our religious life are becoming, and how many churches are well content to dwell alone and plan for their own benefit, while the poor are not welcome among them. I know how easy is the sway of selfishness, and how seductive. The problems of society are difficult, and it is easy for Christians to evade responsibility for them by pleading that they are doing something better than attend to them, by preaching the gospel of eternal life. So on many sides I meet the danger that the Christian people may not act after the manner of Jesus in dealing with their fellow-men, in this solemn day when the problems of the life of man with man are as urgent as they are obscure. And all these fears I entertain by the side of my thankfulness for all the living faith, and all the frank open-mindedness, and all the warm and helpful love, that I behold in the Christian people and joyfully acknowledge as the work of God in them.

I am not speaking here to a company of the Christian people: I am addressing a company of sincere and high-minded human beings, devoted to the work of education. It is a company in which a Christian man has honorable standing if he deserves it, and a non-Christian man has the same on the same terms. Not as Christians or as non-Christians therefore do I address my auditors. All the more freely for this reason can I speak to them all; and to my present audience I have a message. The Christian people are among us, and, with all their faults, have proved themselves a good gift of God to mankind. Our world needs them now, and needs to have them at their best and strongest. It never needed them more, for they stand for that high spiritual life and meaning which the present world is in great danger of forgetting. Yet here they stand, in this trying transition-age, surrounded by subtle dangers. To all who hear me in this honorable company I appeal, and I say, Help us Christian people of your own generation to fulfil our calling. Whatever your own beliefs may be, help us to be what we ought. Help us to open our minds. Press on with your work of enlarging the boundaries of knowledge. Make clear and intelligible and irresistible whatever you discover, and urge it upon us with all persistency. Keep your own tempers sweet, in order that you may the better commend to us what we need to receive from you. Be candid with us, in order that we may have confidence in you and learn the better from you. Teach us the truth of the time, and teach us so wisely and in so fair a spirit that we cannot but receive what you have to offer us. Thus help us to open our minds. Help us also, I beg not less earnestly, to hold our faith, — for even this service does not lie beyond your reach. Do not profess to know that our faith amounts to nothing. Do not claim to be sure that there is no place for faith. Open your minds to that great spiritual secret which philosophy discerns, and upon the confines of which science itself is treading, and of which religion is the revelation. Forbear to scorn our sense of a great, abiding, eternal, spiritual reality, but rather encourage and help us to fill with the thought of God that space which cannot be left vacant without darkening the universe. Help us also to limit faith to the true field of faith. Batter down things that we may try to set up as objects of faith that are not properly such. Hold us to clear speech and honest declaration. Drive us back to our essentials and our simplicities. Make us miserable when we try to defend mere outposts as if they were the citadel. Compel us to assert the few eternal verities, and then join us in setting them by the side of the other certainties that you proclaim to us. And help us also, I entreat, to expand our hearts in sympathetic and helpful love. Reprove us for our selfishness when you behold it, dealing with us in the faithfulness of sorrowful sincerity. Come also and be our fellow-helpers in the field of love. All that is human should care for all that is human, and this field of humanity is as truly yours as ours. Inspire us to emulation of your humanitarian endeavors and successes. Let us together be planning for the larger good of our country and our fellows everywhere. The vast social problems ought to attract us all, whatever we are, and to hold our best attention till we have actually accomplished something for the betterment of the common lot of men. Work with us in the spirit of Jesus: for what better spirit is there for any son of humanity to make his own than his? Thus help us to serve our kind. Whoever is at the front in any good endeavor, let us all encourage him: and together let us hope that the Christian people may rise to their true character, and fulfil the upward movement of their history, and be worthy of their Lord, and do those greater works of love and power which their Master foretold for them in the days when the world's work should be upon their shoulders.

II

THE CHRISTIAN DOCTRINE

The Christian Doctrine begins, of course, with the teaching of the Founder.

Not without reason is Jesus known as the Great Teacher. He was no orator, it is true, nor was he a formal preacher, but rather a quiet converser, a talker among men. Yet he spoke with marvellous power, and made his mark upon the inmost life of his hearers. Never man spoke like him, they said. They felt the authority that moved in his words. Only fragments of his utterance have been preserved to us, but the brief discourses and conversations that we read in the Gospels stand unique in spiritual power among the utterances of the world. They represent a vast mass of teaching, lost to us in form but preserved in its fruits: for out of his spiritual wealth there poured, throughout his ministry, an abundance of spoken truth that remained to perpetuate his influence and serve as the foundation of the Christian doctrine. The early church started upon its way with its memory stored with the rich and fruitful utterances of the Master.

One might think that the Master's utterances would forever stand alone, and would constitute the entire sum of doctrine for Christianity. Who would venture to add, when he had spoken? More especially when the church had come, as it soon did come, to adore him as divine, how could the teaching of any others, especially of his own disciples, be added to what he had given? Yet on the other hand who could be restrained from adding? Jesus had not merely brought into the world a quantity of truth to leave it there: he had opened a perpetual fount of truth, which could not cease to flow. He had given the Christian people a new light on all things. He had shown them how to know the things that are. That process of thinking, learning, and knowing, which is endless for man because it is man's glory, would thenceforth go on, for them, in the light of the truth that he had taught them. By an inevitable and most blessed necessity, his friends would apply what he had shown them to the interpretation of all that they thought or knew. Paul did this, and John. In their teaching they did not merely repeat what Jesus had said: they looked for themselves into the mystery of God and of life, and for themselves they thought out truth in that sublime region. This is what their Master desired them to do, for he came among them to make men of the first order, able to think right and true thoughts about the living God. He still desires the same. We too shall please him best if we humbly, reverently, resolutely, hopefully, think for ourselves, in that region of truth which his mission opens before us.

Thus came into being the Christian doctrine; and we see at once that it was formed from two sources. First came the great contribution of the one Lord himself, the truth that his people had from him. Then was added the contribution of Christian men who saw light in his light, and had visions of the truth of God through his illumination. Christianity began its course rich with the treasure of the Master's utterances, and grew yet richer as it went on, — strange yet glorious to say, — through the diligent and inspired thought of holy men, moved by the Holy Spirit, devoted to the things of God. Both these parts of the primeval doctrine were gathered into the New Testament, which with its immeasurable wealth of living truth is the noble fruit of Christ's presence in the world.

But do not fail to notice how the Christian doctrine came into existence. Do not imagine that it came by being formulated some fine day by the decree of some great council, or by the command or endorsement of authorized men. The teaching of Jesus did not grow into doctrine by being written out and formulated, or by being discussed and officially interpreted. Not all that his apostles said or wrote entered into the substance of the Christian doctrine, nor all that Jesus himself said, either. Doctrine was no such formal, external thing as to take up something merely because it had been said, even though it were by the Lord himself. No, doctrine grew as a vital thing, and grew in the soil of life. The Christian doctrine sprang up in the experience of Christian living. It was the Christian truth as learned by the Christian people; and both elements, the truth and the experience, were essential to the producing of it. Any thought that did not take root in this vital soil, and take root to stay and live, did not come to form a part of the Christian doctrine. The process was simply a vital process of assimilation. Jesus appeared among men, and poured out spiritual truth in great abundance. He poured it out by what he said, by what he did, and by what he was. Words, deeds, and personality all preached: life, death, and resurrection all uttered living and powerful truth. This rich and various utterance that Jesus made fell into the hearing and the hearts of men and women who became the Christian people. Into the very being of these men and women this truth entered, with transforming power, and a new life sprang up in them. By and by it came to pass that this truth from Jesus had filtered through their minds and hearts and life, and come forth to expression on the other side. It is this second expression, this reproduction, this lived-over substance, of the truth that

Jesus brought, that constitutes the Christian doctrine. Nothing properly belongs to the Christian doctrine that has not passed through this process. Not until the Christian people have made the Christian truth their own and given it form from their own experience, does there come to be a Christian doctrine. The contribution of Jesus to mankind became doctrine in his church by passing through the experience to which it gave rise in men, and coming out in the form which that experience gave to it.

Have I made plain how the Christian doctrine came into existence? Is it clear that the truth that Jesus gave became Christian doctrine through the medium of the Christian people and their life? Then it is time to inquire what the contents of this original Christian doctrine are. What was the doctrine, or the experienced, realized, and re-uttered truth, with which Christianity began its course?

Here I know that I touch disputed ground, possibly dangerous ground. There are many opinions as to what the doctrinal stock of the first Christianity was. We are all tempted to count our own doctrines in, and assume that our own form of Christianity is the original. But I think we can reach some reasonably satisfactory answer to the question that has just been asked. If we are careful to keep the question in the form that has now been given to it, I think it can be answered. This is the form: — What truths do we find, that came forth from Jesus, and filtered through the life and experience of the early Christian people, into expression in Christian doctrine? Certainly there are five great truths that stand thus related to Christ and to the experience of his followers. Perhaps there are more: we will judge when we have looked at these. All of these five truths we find uttered by the Master, and uttered again in later time by the disciples as truths now known to them in actual experience.

1. The relation between man and God which Jesus presented as the right relation has come to be experienced, and enters into the doctrine. Jesus the Master said, "When ye pray, say, Our Father who art in heaven." Paul the disciple said, out of the common experience, "We have not received the spirit of bondage, again unto fear, but we have received the spirit of adoption, whereby we cry, Abba, Father." The truth, proclaimed by Jesus, that man may enter into filial and family relations with the good and holy God, has now been experienced by the Christian people, and has come forth from their glad filial life at home with God, into permanent expression. The Christian people have found the secret of life, in finding themselves sons to God. This experienced relation is the fundamental element in the Christian life, and in the Christian doctrine. No

one title represents the whole idea, but at the centre it is a doctrine of the Fatherhood of God.

2. The significance of the coming and work of Jesus himself has been learned by experience, and enters into the doctrine. The Master said, "Come unto me, all ye that labor and are heavy-laden, and I will give you rest." The disciple, speaking out of the common experience, said, "Being justified by faith, we have peace with God through our Lord Jesus Christ, through whom we have had our access by faith into this grace wherein we stand." To the early church, Christ is the way, and the truth, and the life. He has laid down his life for the sheep as the true and faithful shepherd: he is the Saviour of men, able to save them to the uttermost who come unto God by him. His place is that of the restorer, the bringer of men home to God, the one in whom we have our spiritual life and welfare. This rela-

tion between Christ and men is not a theoretical one, but an actual: it is experienced, it is known in the life. Through the Christian experience has come forth in vital power the doctrine of the Saviourhood of Jesus Christ.

3. The Spirit whom Jesus promised has been experienced as a present reality, and this reality has entered into doctrine. Jesus said, " I will send you another Helper, that he may abide with you forever, even the Spirit of truth." Paul responds, out of the common experience, " The Spirit himself bears witness with our spirit, that we are children of God. As many as are led by the Spirit of God, they are God's sons." The gift of the indwelling divine has become a real gift, blessedly known in inward experience, and proved by its fruits. There is an indwelling divine which is the inspiration of faith and hope and love to the Christian people, and the fruit of the Spirit is found

in all the holy graces. The Christian experience has created the doctrine of the reality and the Friendhood of the Spirit.

4. The relation between man and man which Jesus presented as the right one is a relation of love: this relation has begun to be realized, and enters into doctrine. Jesus said, " Thou shalt love the Lord thy God with all thy heart, and thou shalt love thy neighbor as thyself." Paul answered, " Now abideth faith, hope, love, these three; and the greatest of these is love " : and John, " Let us love one another, for God is love." Fellowship is the sweet bond of a living unity among those who have learned of Jesus, and helpfulness is the Christian badge. Experience has made a doctrine of the Supremacy of Love.

5. The high ethical demand of Jesus is beginning to be fulfilled in the life of the Christian people, because here is a power that can fulfil it; and the attainableness of moral victory has entered into doctrine.

Jesus the Master said, commanding and promising at once, "Ye shall be perfect, even as your Father in heaven is perfect." Paul the disciple replies, "The law of the Spirit of life in Christ Jesus has delivered me from the law of sin and death." "The fruit of the light is in all goodness and righteousness and truth." In Christ good men are made. He required goodness, after the pattern and inspiration of the eternal good, and he brings it to pass, by the strong holy operation of the indwelling Spirit. In the Christian holiness, imperfect though it is, that goodness which Christ required and promised is actually emerging in the world. Promises to "him that overcometh" will in due time be claimed. What should enter into doctrine if not this? Experience has taught the church to hold with joy the doctrine of the Transforming Power.

All this, I am sure, is true. Here are five great realities that had come from

Christ into experience, and come from experience to be assured possessions of the Christian people. Five great realities: the Fatherhood of God, the Saviourhood of Jesus Christ, the Friendhood of the Spirit, the Supremacy of Love, and the Transforming Power. The assertion of these realities forms the main stock of doctrine in the early Christianity. I doubt whether there were any other truths that deserve to rank with these, though doubtless there are other truths implied in these. If there is any other that ranks with these, it is the sublime affirmation of immortality. This was not exactly a truth made known by Jesus, or a possession peculiar to his followers. Yet it was one of their possessions, gained as their own in fresh fulness and power in their experience with him. One element in that inspiring Christian life which made existence new to so many of the poor and unfortunate of this world was the exhilaration that came with the sense of deathlessness. Men now expected to live forever, continuing in Christ himself, and with him, that life in which they were now most blessed: and who can wonder that the world was new? But I think the sense of immortality came rather as a conclusion or corollary from the Christian doctrine than as a primary part of it; and I think that the Christian doctrine itself, defined as that which came from Christ by way of experience, and was held and proclaimed as the characteristic truth of Christianity, consisted chiefly in the affirmation of these five great realities as realities, namely, — the Fatherhood of God and the filial life with him; the Saviourhood of Jesus Christ by whom we have been brought home to God; the Friendhood of the Spirit who dwells in us; the Supremacy of Love as the law of life and duty; and the Transforming Power of the divine grace, whereby God is able to do exceeding abundantly above all that we ask or think, in the production of real goodness, according to the power that is at work in us already.

Now we turn to another part of our subject. From this glorious body of doctrine, or of truth experienced, began the long history of the Christian doctrine, continuing till now. About this I must say two or three things, important to the present purpose.

I need not show that the history of Christian doctrine will be a history of divine realities, handled by human thought. Here again, the divine seed is cast forth into the field of the world, to be received as it may by the soil that awaits it and the influences that are around. Human thought deals with the divine realities as it can. God's truth takes its chances of being fairly or unfairly considered, wisely or unwisely interpreted, rightly or wrongly grouped. The result must be a mixed result, noble but imperfect. Any one who expects the Christian doctrine at any given time to be wholly clear, consistent, and harmonious with the mind of God, has not considered the whole case. When divine realities are handled by human thought, we can predict a mixed result, noble but imperfect, and imperfect in a multitude of ways.

See how variation comes in. There is an open door for it at once, and in it comes. The open door for variation is explanation. The great primary element in the doctrine is not explanation, or theory, but assertion, the assertion of the reality. The church proclaims that God is our Father, that Christ is our Saviour, that the Spirit is the indwelling Friend, that love is the law of life, that victory is possible. The strength and vigor of the doctrine lies in the confident holding and affirmation of these realities. As long as the Christian people are firmly holding these things for true, so long is the doctrine a living and glowing thing, competent to win its way by inherent energy. But it seems inevitable that efforts should be made to explain these great realities, to account for them to the judgment of man, to tell just how and why they are true. No one can say that this tendency is wrong. The things of God are infinitely worthy of the thought of man, and it is a high human glory to gaze into them and seek to understand. But who does not see that variety of views will come in, as soon as the effort to explain is made? Minds, tempers, training, degrees of sympathy, opportunities to know, abilities for understanding, power of expression, all differ, and variation in doctrine is inevitable, when once the enterprise of explanation has been launched.

All the more because of another tendency, namely, the tendency to regard the explanation that is reached as part and parcel of the doctrine itself, thenceforth inseparable from it. By virtue of this tendency, with which we are all familiar, every inquirer as to the how and the wherefore of the divine realities becomes himself a contributor to the substance of the doctrine. The legislature makes the law, but the court interprets it; and the court's interpretation is accepted as part and parcel of the law. So, given the divine reality, fascinating in its mysteriousness, and the explanation or theory of it that is accepted becomes attached to the reality as a part of it. The theory may be good or bad, wise or foolish, it makes no difference. The holder of the theory calls it the doctrine, always, and to him the two are one. But when there are many inquirers, all fascinated by the glory of God in his truth, and all sincerely explaining its mysteries as best they may, variation in doctrine needs not to be announced, for it will come, welcome or unwelcome, and will come to stay. If my neighbor and I, believing, for example, in the transforming power and the victorious holiness, investigate the mode and means of the victory, and he reaches one conception and I another, then to each of us the doctrine will consist of the great reality plus his own explanation of it, and there will be two doctrines of holiness, one his and one mine.

I do not think for a moment that this process can be avoided. This is a part of that inevitable to which divine realities submit themselves when they are handled by human thought. I am simply calling attention to the inevitableness of variation in Christian doctrine, and of the entrance of inferior forms of doctrine by the side of better forms. Judgments that are partial, one-sided, temporary, provisional, are certain to be formed, and for the time to be held tenaciously as the only true: but with the lapse of time men will be called to abandon them, however reluctantly, in favor of other views that are truer, even though these in turn are still imperfect. All this is inevitable, when divine realities are handled by human thought. There was no way to keep Christian doctrine from variation, except to keep thought away from it; and that is not God's way with his creatures. So we must not be scandalized if we find the Christian doctrine changing its forms, and seeming sometimes contradictory and inconsistent with itself; nor should we be too superior if we watch this process from the point of view of science. It is the common lot. The Christian truth has fared as all other truth has fared, when human thought dealt with it.

If we wish to understand the Christian doctrine, there is another aspect of its history for us to consider. It is important that we notice through what influences the doctrine of the early past has come down to the present. I have spoken of the certainty of variation and conflicting forms: a few words now about the influences through which the course of the history of the Christian doctrine has run. Three great influences have touched the doctrine, modifying it for good and for evil.

The first was philosophy. It was Greek philosophy that first laid its hand upon the Christian doctrine. The philosopher gained a standing among the exponents of the faith and the interpreters of the doctrine, and kept his standing long. It could not have been otherwise, and it is vain to wish it might have been otherwise. The period of philosophy was a normal and worthy stage in the life of Christianity, and needful help was given by philosophy at a time when nothing else would do. But Dr. Edwin Hatch was right when he called attention to the deep contrast between the Sermon on the Mount and the Nicene Creed. The Sermon on the Mount is direct, simple, practical, religious: the Nicene Creed is metaphysical, abstract, inferential, non-ethical, theological. One sprang from the mind and heart of Jesus Christ, the other from theological inquiry and controversy among his followers. One was intended to set forth the living truth concerning God and man : the other, to guard the truth that had been accepted, and shut out those who could not join in reciting this statement of it. The contrast is both sharp and deep, and there are many other illustrations as clear and keen as this.

The effect of philosophy upon the Christian doctrine, as this illustration shows, was to elaborate it. That process of identifying the interpretation with the doctrine, of which we spoke, had now its apotheosis. Metaphysical discussion took hold upon implied points, and brought them to the surface, and set them at the front. It called attention to implied connections of thought, and insisted upon filling out a consistent statement of the underlying assumptions. In this way it added to the points of doctrine. It multiplied largely the matters which it was held important to believe. We may almost say that philosophy took a simple faith, and left an elaborate system of belief. It added to the bulk of doctrine, but not to its vitality or working vigor. Thus the doctrine passed through a period of large elaboration in the schools of thought: and the effect still remains upon it. The simplest Christian of to-day inherits, in the teaching that he receives, something from the Greek philosophy.

Next comes organization. After the Roman empire had fallen, there rose the new Roman empire, the imperial church. The church as an institution now obtained standing, not only as an exponent of the faith and an interpreter of the doctrine, but by and by as the sole exponent and interpreter. There was now a great governmental system, in which the sacrament-working element was the dominant force. Sacramentalism and governmentalism go naturally together: and in the middle ages all influences conspired to hold the church in the rank and place of authority in the field of doctrine. There was now an organization that claimed the right to guide the doctrine, and finally the right to determine it, by authority from above.

The effect of organization upon the Christian doctrine was to formalize it. Inheriting much from the metaphysical period that preceded, the church went on to build the doctrine into a scholastic system, philosophy and organization now conspiring to introduce method and completeness as the type-giving idea. Out of the sacramental system, too, grew a regular system of straightforward doctrine, setting forth the authority of the church and the way of salvation through the churchly ministries. The vast weight of organization was a burden upon the doctrine of Christianity, as well as upon the Christian life : flexibility was discouraged, rigidity was favored, by the existing conditions. The system has grown, until the head of the organization stands as the infallible teacher, and the doctrine is solely as he proclaims or sanctions it. Organization has been the formalizer of doctrine. In the love for system and the leaning on authority, all our modern theology inherits something from the great formalizing organization of the middle ages.

Last of the three stands individualism. In the modern age, from the sixteenth century on, Christianity has had to do with the intense individualism that has given character to the west. The Reformation of the sixteenth century was the blossoming-out of individualism, the emerging of personal freedom and responsibility from beneath the churchly sway, the establishing of free and active thought as the method and activity of the age. In our part of the world, Christianity has been under this influence now for four centuries.

I am at a loss for a single word to describe the effect of the modern individualism upon the Christian doctrine, and yet the effect is plain enough. In the age of individualism the interest in the bringing-out of doctrine has certainly increased, and the doctrine has grown sharp and intense. The individualizing impulse is full of life: it imparts freshness, courage, vigor, hopefulness, to all intellectual endeavor. The impulse of the Reformation has stimulated the investigation of Christian truth, and thrown abundant life into the study of the doctrine. But it has also led to division and variety, beyond all precedent. It has differentiated and diversified doctrine, and scattered it, and broken it into fragments. Why not? When we are all free to think, and all do think, each one just as he is, with his own outfit of powers and training, how can all think alike? If we interpret the Christian realities each in his own way, we shall differ in our results. And if, as the case has been, our individualism takes form in a host of organizations, each deeming itself set for the defence of some view of the doctrine, then all the more certainly will the doctrine be diversified and scattered into portions. Still more will this come to pass when the age of individualism inherits from the methods of philosophy and the habits of a scholastic period. The church of Rome is right when it tells us that our Protestantism does not tend to intellectual agreement. The more serious and interesting the matters that we inquire about, the less likely are we to reach identity in the result. The modern individualism has added immensely to the energy of thought upon the Christian doctrine, but not as yet has it brought unity in conclusions: nor will it bring such unity, except by the aid of more spiritual influences. It has been a quickener of doctrine, but a divider also.

I have spoken long enough of the road over which the Christian doctrine has come down to us from its far beginnings. Divine reality, thrown into the living experience of the Christian people, has been to them the theme of thought. The actual reality has been largely the same to them all, but difference and variety in views of it have followed, by an absolute necessity. The doctrine has been elaborated by philosophy, formalized by organization, and quickened but diversified by individualism, and at last, out of the long process, it has come down to us, and stands before us to be estimated as to its value. What is its present worth? How well and justly does it represent those divine realities with which it started? Can we point to it as helpful to the purpose of our apologetics? Is it worthy to stand as a commendation of Christianity? Is it a real help in our presentation of our religion to the world? Wherein does it need improvement? and can we do anything to add to its quality and power? All these questions we have a right to ask, and to them we desire a true answer.

That Christian doctrine concerning which we now make these inquiries is of course the resultant from all the past. We inherit from all our predecessors. On every point of doctrinal belief, the popular thought of to-day inherits more or less from all past theories and interpretations. Our present Christian doctrine contains the old and ever new divine realities, and it contains the many and various results of the handling of them by human thought.

All together these elements, various and incongruous, have come down to us. It could not be otherwise, and it is vain for us to imagine that it has been otherwise. We have not merely what our Master taught, but what the mighty past has given us.

This statement sounds to some, I doubt not, as if I felt constrained chiefly to acknowledge the faults of the process, and to confess the defilements that have come from the touch of man upon the divine realities. But it is not so. I do not feel constrained to set the faults in any such rank. I see a wonder on the other side. The first thing that I have to say about the present Christian doctrine is that the divine realities are still here. They have come down to us. They live, and have their power. The realities that composed the Christian doctrine at the beginning compose it now. All the explaining and difference and variation, all the elaborating by philosophy and formalizing by churchly organization and scattering by modern thought, has not destroyed them as the treasure of the Christian people. Still do these same divine realities hold their place as the centre and substance of the Christian doctrine.

Do you say that I cannot prove it? It is true that it is not a matter for demonstration, but it is a matter for affirmation that cannot be successfully challenged. If I were asked as an observer of my own time what are the essential elements in the Christian doctrine as it now exists, what should I say? What ought I to say? What would any well-informed man say? I should say that first of all it is held by the Christian people that in Christ the true and right relation between man and God, the relation of children with their father, is realized. I should say that the Christians still claim to be living in sonship to God, according to the teaching of

Jesus, and that this experience is their glory. I should even say that the fulness of the meaning of God's fatherhood is now dawning with unprecedented power upon the Christian people. I should say next, that Christians hold unshakenly to the Saviourhood of Jesus Christ. He it is that has brought them home to God and introduced them to that filial life in which they rest and are strong. In his wonderful mission and life, culminating in his wonderful death so rich in sacrifice, the Christian people find the way of their salvation. I should say further that the Christian people experience and acknowledge the Friendhood of the holy indwelling Spirit. They still declare their experience and belief of a present God, a God within them, renewing, transforming, strengthening, fulfilling in actual life the saving purpose of Jesus Christ. I should say that the Christians hold, though all of them imperfectly, to the supremacy of love as the ruling and decisive element in all true character. The experimental presence and possession of a noble and self-forgetful love is nothing unknown, or even rare, among the Christian people, and the ideal of excellence among them is the character that is crowned by love in its purest and sweetest forms. And I should affirm that the Christian people hold that in Christ there is a genuine transforming power, a power of God unto salvation, able to produce a successful holiness. They believe that through Christ it is possible for men to be cleansed of their actual evil, not merely in some theoretical and supposititious way, but really and forever, and brought to actual and positive holiness in the sight of God. And if the affirmation of immortality be considered an essential part of the Christian doctrine, then I should add that the present Christian people hold to immortality as their human birthright and their Christian inheritance, and live in the light of the immortal hope.

Here are all the essential realities of the primitive Christian doctrine; and I affirm that they are held as facts of life and experience now, and proclaimed as present doctrine. After all the centuries they are here, in vitality and power, holding the place in the church that they held at first. They constitute the doctrine, too, not of some small part of the Christian people, but of the mass. I have not recited the creed of some sect, I have uttered the doctrine of Christendom. I have spoken the ecumenical creed.

After what has been said, no one will suppose that I am claiming for this primitive and ecumenical doctrine a perfect, an ideal, a satisfactory hold upon the Christian people. Most freely do I confess to serious imperfections in the holding of this noble sum of Christian doctrine. What would you expect? Have not the divine realities come down, through ages of human handling, to the hands of a generation as imperfect as any of its predecessors? Defects? Certainly, they are here. The most exacting parts of the doctrine are held least satisfactorily, as they always have been. The Christian people are still too unwilling to let their doctrine have its way with their lives, and exercise upon them its searching and cleansing power. They still have much to learn as to the simplicity, the meaning, and the vitality of what they believe. Nowhere, either, is the whole equally well believed and illustrated; for one side is seen and received more clearly in one quarter and another in another, even as it has always been. Moreover, in the long course of transmission the doctrine has become far too various and far too complicated. Around each one of the great divine realities there has gathered a mass of differing and conflicting interpretations; and still the practice persists of confounding these interpretations with the divine reality itself. Thus the people's minds are burdened with a superfluous mass of what they sincerely believe to be Christian doctrine, but of what belongs outside the central field and ought to be separated from the essential matter. There often appears to be deep and irreconcilable conflict between those who hold the reality in common; yet the conflict relates to the explanation of the reality, not to the reality itself. There is great need of learning to distinguish between the realities that the Christian doctrine affirms and the explanations of them in which the history of doctrine abounds. All these things, and doubtless more, must be acknowledged by way of defect in the holding of the Christian doctrine by the Christian people of to-day. Nevertheless, when all the defects have been freely admitted, I still affirm that the great divine realities that made up the Christian doctrine in the beginning make up the Christian doctrine now. I declare that the Christian people throughout the world are believing in the Fatherhood of God, the Saviourhood of Jesus Christ, the Friendhood of the Spirit, the supremacy of love, and the reality of the transforming power of the divine grace. They diverge widely in their explanation of these facts, and in the views that they associate with them; they differ widely in the forms of experience to which these facts give rise; but in the facts themselves they all believe, and it is this belief that makes them Christians. And this presence in the world of the original body of Christian doctrine, existing still not in theory alone but in experience as an inspiring and renewing force, I hail with joy as a proof of the presence of God in the history of mankind.

I am well aware that there are many who make little account of the presence of this body of central doctrine. From two quarters I may be criticised for setting it forth as so important a thing. An objector, from without the Christian circle, may say, "Ah, but this is not Christianity. Historically, Christianity includes a thousand varieties, so many and so mutually contradictory that one cannot even determine what it claims to be. You may find a few peculiarities in common, as you are doing now, but that is of no consequence. The historical Christian doctrine is a far more complex and difficult thing than this, and it is not a fact that the whole can be gathered up into a few statements." And some earnest soul within the Christian circle may perhaps unwittingly join hands with the objector from without, when he hears so short a creed pronounced, and one that does not contain some theories or explanations that seem to him to be of the first importance. "Of what avail," he may say, "is the common acceptance of a few mere central facts, when almost all who are said to accept them are wrong in their understanding of them? Agreement on facts that are variously understood is only the shadow of agreement. The substance of agreement lies in the understanding of the facts, and unity in this is wanting. So what is the use of proclaiming as ecumenical doctrine a body of realities that all interpret differently, and the most misinterpret?"

But I think I have been right in my statement of what the Christian doctrine really is, namely, that it consists in divine realities handled by human thought. This ought to dispose of the first objection. If this is true, the objector ought not to be asking that we take all the variations of doctrine into the common stock and insist upon holding them all as a part of our present Christianity. It is somewhat like asking that the present science of physics or chemistry should include all the theories of past days, or that philosophy herself should muster her dead along with her living, and defend the views of her former magnates as adequate to the present time. Let us have sense. If we have the original and abiding realities of the Christian faith held to-day as Christian doctrine, we have what all our fathers have had, in every generation; and if we interpret them variously among ourselves and differ in our conception of them, we do what all our fathers did, and what all our children must do, as long as it is the nature of man to know in part. Christianity consisted at first in certain great abiding facts of spiritual life and experience. It consists now in the same. There have been a thousand thoughts and theories about it, that enter into the history of it but form no permanent part of it, and we are by no means bound to reckon them all in when we wish to know what the Christian doctrine really is. And the same answer may serve when we meet the objection that comes from within the Christian circle. It is not necessary for me to find my theory of the manner of the Saviourhood of Christ, for example, accepted in the universal thought of Christendom, in order for me to perceive, and to rejoice, that all Christendom believes in the Saviourhood of Christ. My theory of that great reality is the best that I can form at present, but it certainly is not faultless. If my theory of the Saviourhood of Christ must be accepted in order for men to be saved, most Christians would be lost, for the most have not accepted it. What is true of my theory is true of yours, whatever it may be. There is no one explanation of that great reality upon which most of those who have trusted in Christ for salvation have agreed. So great a fact is sure to have its many interpretations, differing as minds differ; and those who find eternal life in the Saviourhood of Christ may well rejoice that those who understand it differently from them find eternal life in it too. We are all pupils in the school of Christ, handling divine realities in human thought that is half-trained and half-sanctified at the best, and our interpretations are like those of our fathers, neither full nor final. And so we are confirmed in thinking that the great experimental realities of Christianity provide the genuine abiding elements in the Christian doctrine. Through these comes the life in which Christianity consisted at first and consists always. And these central verities do certainly form the heart of the universal Christian doctrine as it is held to-day. They are now experienced, and now proclaimed as verities that Christ brought near and experience has confirmed.

Of the now-existing Christian doctrine, therefore, I am by no means ashamed. I am not here to apologize for it. It is the most precious of the products of the past.

In the mission of Christ, God sent it forth into the world, and the long movement of history has borne it on to us. I wish that it were better understood in its simplicity; I wish that preachers might learn to distinguish between it and what surrounds it; I wish that it were held by the Christian people with better conviction and more faithful obedience to its supreme demands. There are conceptions and presentations of it for which I might be constrained to apologize, if the occasion arose. But of the Christian doctrine itself I am not ashamed, and for it I have no apologies to offer. It was a great gift of God at first, and it remains a great and worthy gift of God to-day. If those who hold it can but walk worthy of it, and commend it to general confidence by their proclamation of its truths, the whole world will have reason to thank God for it as a present gift of blessing.

What can we do for the Christian doctrine, we may ask, to render it more effective in the present world? What can be done for it must be done mainly through the Christian people; and the need of the Christian people with reference to their doctrine lies just where our present course of thought is leading us. The exceeding preciousness and the supreme value of this central body of experimental truth, — this is what the Christian people need to learn. The permanent element in the doctrine consists in the declaration of the great experimental truths: the changing and passing element consists in the various interpretations of those truths, made from time to time in human thought. We are so devoted to the interpretations that we often lose our sense of the vitality of the facts. We need to be called back to the realities, where the power dwells. I well remember how like a cobweb-brushing breeze a statement of the late Robert

William Dale many years ago swept through my mind. It stood at the front of a treatise of his upon the Atonement, which I was beginning to read. "It is not the doctrine of the death of Christ that atones for human sin, but the death itself." That power resides in a reality, and not in any doctrine of a reality, — this, it would seem, I might have known before, so simple is it, and so obviously true. We need to see it concerning the whole body of Christian doctrine. Theories and explanations of the great realities we must form, and hold, always hoping to correct and enrich them as we go on. No one is asking us to lay them down and leave them, for that to most of us is impossible. But it is in the good God our Father, not in any doctrine of his Fatherhood, that we have our filial life at home with him. It is by our living Saviour Jesus Christ that we are brought home to God, not through some doctrine of him, or some doctrine of the manner of his Saviourhood. It is the indwelling Spirit himself that helps our weakness, and we are strengthened by his real touch, not by a doctrine of the Spirit, or of his personality, or of his relations in the Godhead. It is by love, and not by a doctrine of love, that we are to prove ourselves Christians. The experience of the transforming power is what we want, and without this ever so good a theory of the transforming power is powerless. If we attain to such a view of the Christian doctrine as this, we can declare that the great realities are quick and powerful now, as confidently and strongly as could the apostles themselves when the faith was new.

I count upon two helps toward a better conception of the Christian doctrine. I expect valuable help from the clear and straightforward thinking that is characteristic of the best intellectual work of our time. It is necessary that the Christian

people learn to distinguish things that
differ, and thus get their doctrine clear of
complication with what does not belong to
it. In this they need to learn from such
intellectual work as is done in this university, and wherever men set themselves
to the task of clear thinking and discernment of things as they are. Help us, I
say to-day as I said yesterday. Go on
with clear thinking. Establish the right
way of mental work as the only way that
shall be welcome anywhere. Illustrate
sound, strong thinking for us, until it shall
be a matter of course that we must make
it our own. Make it impossible for us to
live thinking confusedly and incorrectly.
Every advance in good intellectual practice
helps Christian doctrine toward the day of
disentanglement and independence. It
leads on toward the time when the Christian realities shall be distinguished in all
minds from theories concerning them, and
the power of the divine reality can go forth

in its simplicity to influence minds prepared to receive it.

The other help that I count upon can come only from within the Christian people. There is nothing but religious life that can most powerfully strengthen the cause of religion in the world. It is life that begets life. Only the genuine experience of the divine grace and life, — such experience as the first Christians had, and all the best of their successors, — only this can bring the help that is most needful. But I see it coming. Already, in our own time, we find a fresh insistence upon genuineness and reality in religion. Words are powerless by themselves, preaching that rings hollow is unwelcome, phrases empty of life do not convince, churches are blamed for professions that do not rule the life. The demand for genuineness thus far appears largely in negative form, clearing away the ungenuine; and to many it seems dangerous and destructive. But it will not continue to be negative. It is a hopeful beginning for a deeper experience of the great realities of the Christian faith. A generation that insists upon tearing down the false will not be content until the true has been built up in its place. The experience of God, of Christ, of the Spirit, of love, and of victory is coming in. It will take new forms, but it will be the old reality, and the Christian doctrine will stand forth strong and clear, —clear in the light of simplicity, and strong in the strength of God.

III

THE CHRISTIAN POWER

IF we have a people and a doctrine, what more do we want to make up our Christianity? A set of ideas satisfactory and inspiring, and a multitude of people devoted to them, — is not this enough? Many suppose, or assume, that this will account for it all. When we have seen these two elements, and acknowledged them, have we not seen all that there is of it? But we have something more. Our discernment of the real nature of Christianity is not complete till we have apprehended and in some degree understood the Christian Power.

The Christian power is not a late-coming element. We see it from the first. We perceive it at work in the very production of the Christian people and the Christian doctrine. There was an initial power, that brought forth these two great facts in the world, and this power we can trace without difficulty. It began, as we know, in the Master, Jesus himself, and the qualities by which he made his impression. He drew to himself the first disciples, by the joint influence of his marvellous personality and the high, helpful, and inspiring truth that he offered them. Virtue went forth from him, upon such as could receive it. His " Follow me " was powerful, and his instruction was enlightening, uplifting, transforming. His time for work was very short, and only beginnings were possible in his brief lifetime, and yet he left behind him in the world a group of human beings spiritually changed by the touch of his personality, and instructed in the first principles of his truth. Thus Jesus became the creator of the Christian people, by the power that was in him. It was a personal power, awakening, reproving, consoling, spiritualizing, opening heaven over the earth for men.

After his departure, there came upon his friends a mighty visitation of spiritual energy. It was not associated merely with their remembrances of his life and words among them, but rather with the divine surprise that his resurrection brought upon them. Now they looked up to him as exalted to the right hand of God in glory; and along with this thought of the glory that had been given to him there came upon them an immense and overwhelming influence, an inspiration of the divine Spirit, and an energy of faith beyond all precedent. The evidence of it is not found alone in the narrative of the occurrences of the Day of Pentecost, in the Acts of the Apostles. Some think that narrative is not historical. But if that narrative were not there, the story of the early Christianity as a whole would still conclusively imply some such experience as is there described, — an enlargement of spiritual vision, a quickening of confidence, a visitation of power. The history cannot be accounted for without the descent of the Holy Spirit upon the church. Somehow there came in those days an amazing outburst of enthusiastic certainty, a rush of vigor, a transforming conviction of the great realities, by which neophytes became heralds and expounders of the faith, and a scattered little flock became a strong people. Out of this visitation of power came, in due time, the missionary impulse, and the new faith went out to the wide Roman world. Thus it was that the power made the people.

It was through the same experience of power that the Christian doctrine was born. The doctrine, we may remember, was not merely the truth, but the truth as the church knew it by experience. It consisted in the Christian conceptions after they had passed through the medium of the Christian life, and had thus become vital possessions of the Christian people. Nothing but the immense vitality of the experience could have brought the doctrine forth as a living thing. We greatly misjudge if we think the adoption of the Christian doctrine was the cool adoption of a set of opinions : it was the glowing realization of a world of spiritual verities. Herein was manifested a tremendous power, and Christianity was already signalized in the world as a living force of great energy.

The power has continued until now, and we have to note that it has wrought in the same manner as the other elements of Christianity that we have considered. It was cast forth into the human world, and its operation was affected by its field and modified by what it had to work upon. It has wrought steadily on, age after age, and yet for its results it has been compelled to bide its time and gain by gradual increments. James Hinton, who had ideas of his own about Nature as an expression of God, — ideas fine in æsthetic quality, searching in moral power, and most valuable, as he conceived, for practical life, and at the same time thoroughly revolutionary, — once estimated the time that would have to be allowed for the introduction of such ideas to full effective application. He put the period at two hundred years, with judgment that it would be longer rather than shorter. First, the idea must be seen in enthusiastic vision by some one, and enunciated for the world to hear. It must get abroad among men, and be somewhat widely considered. It must come to be deemed important. Then it must be ignored, recognized, restated, ridiculed, refuted, denied, doubted, admitted, discussed, affirmed, believed, accepted, taught to adults, taught to children, wrought into literature, put into practice, taught to another generation of children, kept in practice, tested by its fruits, allowed to modify other ideas, embodied in institutions; and in the course of some generations it will sink in among the certainties that are assumed and acted upon without question and without thought. For this process two hundred years is a short period. This is a fair illustration of the kind of world in which Christianity was cast abroad as seed upon the field. We are often asked, almost triumphantly, why Christianity has not accomplished more in so very long a time. But there is no such thing as long time or short time, absolutely. Everything is relative, and time is long or short according to what has to be accomplished in it. Time that is long for one purpose is short for another. Time that is long for a national career may be short for the lifetime of an idea. No deeply significant periods in human history are short: all great movements are long movements. I have a friend, a geologist, who affirms that every minister ought to take a course in historical geology, in order to learn something about the length of processes, and thus at once enlarge and slow down his expectations of divine operation among men. Certainly a just perspective in history will tend to cure us of much of our hurry, and silence many of our cavils. Christianity undertook a moral transformation in an evil world. It must be judged in the light of slow processes and long periods.

Thinking in this strain, we shall not wonder or be scandalized at the great reaction that we are often asked to notice, at the end of the first age of power, when the apostles had departed. That such a reaction and decline of energy occurred is certain. Yet it was not so much a reaction of Christianity, as it was a reaction of human nature after its first leap of new life. Human kind never puts forth exceptional energy without paying for it in reaction, and the vigor of the first Christian period was followed by comparative lifelessness in the second. Nor can we wonder that when Christianity grew up in the larger world, after its transplantation, its power seemed hampered and repressed by its surroundings and materials. All this was of the inevitable. Nor, on the other hand, do we wonder when we see again and again the breaking-forth of genuine and effective power in unexpected quarters. This was the reassertion of the native quality. The history of the Christian power is simply the long illustration of these two opposites.

The history of the Christian power opens a field too vast to be entered now. I cannot even enumerate at all the works of usefulness and help in which that power has been manifested. Only the briefest statement can now be made, a statement of the simple fact that through its history

Christianity has shown itself possessed of true vitality and vast energy; that though it has been resisted, and its force has been diminished, so that it had its days of comparative weakness, it has nevertheless proved itself to be animated by a genuine and most vital power. This is a commonplace, and as a commonplace I shall let it stand. It ought to be unquestioned. I do not believe, let it be said in passing, in claiming for Christianity all the good that has been done within its field. Extravagant claims defeat themselves. It is not true that to Christianity alone we should attribute all the progress of that part of the world which it has influenced. Let us be fair to other forces in society, and to the general movement of God in history. Yet Christianity has been a potent factor in the great improvement. To its influence we can fairly and justly trace large gains in the general good. It has sweetened the universal life, in a thousand ways. It has been influential in the mitigating of cruelties, the abolishing of barbarities, the delivering of the enslaved, the lifting-up of the downtrodden, and the long movement toward giving to all their rights. In spite of its own special entanglements and embarrassments, and the frequent discrediting of its influence and value through the faults of its friends, it has done its good work, and abundantly vindicated itself as a living and beneficent force.

There are some who are ready to tell us that the power that we associate with the name of Christ is mainly in the past. They admit that he has been great, but claim that other lords now hold sway, and he is passing into forgetfulness. There were different days once, in what we call the ages of faith, when men were simpler and more easily satisfied. Then Christ was influential, and was sufficient to the world that then was. But now we demand more evidence for what we are to receive, and accept nothing with the ancient readiness ; and under the new requirements Christ fails to be vindicated, and his power is gone. But these judges of events are strangely astray in their perceptions. The truth is that in what we call the ages of faith the largeness of the power of Christ was scarcely even suspected, still less put to the test of life. It is only now that the searching and glorious meaning of his spiritual power is beginning to be perceived. It is deep injustice to the present age to declare that it is no longer looking to Jesus with reverence and sense of dependence. Our age is not leaving Christ out of sight and memory. Its method of recognizing his power differs from that of other days, and much that has been associated with him may now have lost the reverence that once was given to it. But if we ask to whom or to what the world is looking to-day, in its deepest and most earnest heart, for spiritual light and counsel, there is but one answer. It is looking to Jesus. To the powerful simplicity of his truth and the efficient strength of his leadership the world is even now turning as its best hope. There is weakness and fault enough in this, I know, and there is too much forgetfulness of his precepts and his spirit. The worldly impulse is always with us, ready to sweep men and nations off into disloyal selfishness and pride. Nevertheless it is recognized as it never was before, that whether we are willing to act upon it or not, the spirit of Jesus is the only spirit that can work peace and righteousness among men and nations, and that in him, if we would let him have his way, there is actual power to right our wrongs and heal our woes. His personality stands out impressive and revered, and there is to-day a devotion to the real Christ, in work and service, such as no other age has known. The power still lives. Sometimes with an enthusiastic joy, and sometimes with a pathetic confidence, our own time turns to him who is the voice of God among us, uttering with authority the word of power and hope.

One transparent and triumphant evidence of the strength and persistence of the Christian power is ever before us. It resides in this, that in all the ages the Christian people and the Christian doctrine have been kept in the world, and kept possessed in good degree of their characteristic vitality. That the Christian people are still here, and in spite of all imperfections are still bearing essentially the Christian character, we know quite well. It is equally true that the doctrine of to-day is essentially the doctrine of the beginning, and that it still persists in its original character, as spiritual reality experienced. It has come down to us not merely as a set of ideas, but as a set of ideas wrought into life and in life persisting; and the realities experienced and the

life persisting are the same as at the first.
I said that some power originally produced
the Christian people and the Christian
doctrine, and gave the doctrine to the
people as a factor in their life. Now I
add that some power, in spite of all diffi-
culties and failures, has kept them in the
world till now. The good seed was cast
into a thorn-field, and yet there is a har-
vest, after many days. In human affairs
there has been much to dissipate the
Christian energy, to depress its operation
and to injure its fruits. It has met indif-
ference and opposition without, and mis-
conception, unfaithfulness, lukewarmness,
sometimes treachery, within, and yet the
power has kept its product in existence,
and has not lost its hold upon mankind.
Differences in the age and imperfections
in the product often conceal the fact, but
the fact is that we have here and now, and
throughout the Christian world, essentially
the same realities in human experience

that appeared among the friends of Jesus immediately after his departure. There has been a power sufficient to preserve them until now.

This is all that I must take time to say upon the history of the Christian power. Such facts of course bring their question. What is the most probable source of the Christian power? Why was it, we are led to ask, that the Christian people sprang up, and came out into history with the Christian truth fused into doctrine in their experience? What has caused the wide usefulness of Christianity in the world? Why has it so deeply satisfied the needs of man? Why has it so often been able to overcome scepticism and establish faith? What has kept the people and the doctrine in the world till now? and wherein lies the present strength of Christianity? Whence, in a word, comes the Christian power?

When I answer this question as I think it should be answered, what will you accuse me of? If you accuse me of begging the question, I shall deny the validity of the charge. If you accuse me of making it all too simple, at that I shall not be troubled. I have long since learned that the true is the simple, and that we human beings have wasted centuries, all told, in devising needlessly complicated explanations of things. If my explanation is simple, simple let it be; and if you intend to object to it, object on some better ground than that.

My answer is that the most reasonable account of the power of Christianity is that Christianity is true. This is the most natural explanation that can be given of that strong, effective, victorious power which certainly appeared in the first days of our faith, which has been fighting its enemies ever since, and which still remains upon the field.

This answer is certainly very short. To one who does not at once accept it, it sounds like begging the question. That is just because it is so short and compact, and the meaning of it has not been brought out. I should be most unwilling to leave it thus curt and unexpanded, for there is need of unfolding its meaning if it is to be received as a true answer. We may not all mean the same thing when we say that Christianity is true. I presume there are many who have used the expression, some accepting it and some rejecting, who have never distinctly asked themselves what they meant by it. In many minds, both of believers and of unbelievers concerning Christianity, there is no clear idea of what it is for Christianity to be true. There are so many definitions of Christianity implied in the thoughts of different persons, the central realities are surrounded by so great a variety of explanations and additions, and the short word "true" may mean so many things, that it is no wonder if ambiguity hangs over the main idea, and we may differ widely without knowing it, as to what we mean by saying that Christianity is true. I am anxious that the right meaning of this central assertion may be clearly perceived. If we understand it, we can judge whether I am right in assigning the truth of Christianity as the best explanation of its power.

What is it, then, for Christianity to be true? When any one affirms that Christianity is true, he means, or ought to mean, that Christianity is made up of realities; that what it represents as real is real; that, in the realm of the soul, things are as it declares that they are; that its affirmations accord with fact, and its experiences are experiences of reality. It is meant that Christianity sets forth the great spiritual realities as they are, and nothing but the test of genuine experiment is needed to prove it.

Notice, I beg, where it is that I thus place the centre of Christianity, and where I take my stand for the purpose of definition. I place the centre of Christianity not in its statements, but in its realities and experiences. I do not identify the truth of Christianity with the statements of its advocates, or any of them, concerning it, or with the explanations that they have offered of its facts, or with the declarations of its creeds, whether special or ecumenical. In all these matters there may be wide and irreconcilable differences. I place the centre of Christianity in its realities and experiences, and there I take my stand for the purpose of definition. For Christianity to be true is for its realities to be realities, experienceable, and experienced. If Christianity is true, it sets forth things that are, in the realm of the soul. It testifies according to truth, concerning the eternal realities.

But this statement in turn needs to be

filled out, for only in the filling-out of it can the proof of it be found. Suppose that Christianity is true: then what is true? What is the truth, or what are the realities, involved? This, after all is our question. We have not told what we mean by saying that Christianity is true, until we have unfolded our statement here, and set before ourselves what it is that is true, or real, in Christianity.

I shall answer the question by reaffirming the elements that compose the Christian doctrine in the experience of the Christian people: and the reaffirmation will not be a waste of words. If Christianity is true, then these great elements entered into it by right, and belong in all right experience of men, because they represent the eternal reality. I hold that Christianity is true: that is, I believe that the great elements that make up the Christian doctrine, by means of the Christian experience, accord with the eternal reality, and rightly represent it. Listen now to the statement of what it is for Christianity to be true.

If Christianity is true, God is the supremely good Being that Jesus declared him to be. He really is at heart a Father to us men, and our right and normal relation to him is that of children living at home with the eternal goodness. When we live as we ought, we shall find ourselves living as true sons, in loyal family fellowship with the best being that the heart of man can conceive. These are the facts, if Christianity is true: this is the kind of God that there is, and there is no other. This is the true and real meaning of existence for us men. The world is the world of such a God, holy and gracious, sin-hating and fatherly. Into the world of such a God, and into life with such a meaning, we are all born, if Christianity is true. It is the duty and the privilege of every one of us to be living at home with the absolutely good and holy God, in filial fellowship: and the better we become acquainted with our God, if Christianity is true, the more thoroughly shall we know him as the perfect and glorious One, in whom all our being finds full rest and satisfaction.

Again, if Christianity is true, Jesus Christ is really the gift of God to us men for our spiritual salvation. He really is for us the way and the truth and the life. He finds us astray in moral evil and brings us home. We were forfeiting in a sinful life our privilege of filial life with the eternal goodness. He came to us to save us out of our sin; and he does bring us out of our sin, into eternal life with God. He really does stand to us as Saviour. In what he has done for us in his life and death there is a genuine reality, rich in blessing for us and for all men. If Christianity is true, Jesus Christ is God's way to us, and our way to God.

Again, if Christianity is true, God is not wholly outside of us, addressing us from beyond ourselves. We have not told the whole when we have said that in Christ he comes to us and seeks us for our good. It is true also that the living God really dwells in our souls. He is a God within. He convinces us of evil by actual inward influence. He really renews our hearts, working character such as he desires to see in us. He truly communes with us in the secret place of the heart. He teaches truth to the soul of man, by real inward suggestion. If Christianity is true, God comes as near to us as we are to ourselves, and we possess him as an actual indwelling companion.

Again, if Christianity is true, the only right inspiration of life and guide of conduct in all relations is what Jesus said it was, — namely, love. The life of sonship toward God is thereby a life of brotherhood toward men. When we live according to love toward our fellows, we do the thing that ought to be, and make of life what life ought to be. When unselfishness and the highest helpful affection form our law of living, then we have struck a chord in the eternal harmony, — and all that is dissonant with love is discord to the eternal harmony. This is the spiritual and practical reality, in this world and in any other world that there may be. This is the thing that is. Here is the clue to the significance of our life, here is the keynote of our duty, here is the true method for all our doings. If Christianity is true, God is love, and all men ought to be love, and existence is successful only so far as existence means love.

And again, if Christianity is true, there is for all of us, corresponding to these spiritual realities, a genuine transforming energy. We are not talking of theories, or supposing cases: we are not discussing far off the good that is to be approved and desired but cannot be attained. Here is a genuine might for action. Here dwells the power of God for salvation. The saving agency of Christ is real, and the indwelling Spirit actually does his work. Transformation is an actual experience, a result attained. Character does become changed when these forces have their way. Sin can be conquered, holiness is possible. High virtue is within our reach, and effective power to do good in the needy world can be had. We can be brought to live at home with God in holy and happy fellowship, and to live in helpful love among men. All this has been done, and can be done again.

If Christianity is true, I say once more, these are the facts in our case, and in the case of all men: this is the thing that is: this is what existence means: when we put reality to the test of sincere experiment, this is what we shall find the genuine and eternal reality to be. For Christianity to be true is for these things to be so, and to be verifiable, and verified, in experience. Let our individual understanding of these realities be adequate or inadequate, that makes no difference with the facts. Though we had no understanding of them at all, nay, though we were totally ignorant of them, these are the facts: this is the kind of world we have been born into: this is what our existence signifies. Though we should disagree widely in our interpretation of these realities, and should even grow so blind in heart as to forget our brotherhood and count one another aliens because of our disagreement, still these are the realities, and these are the realities forever. God is the holy Being with whom we ought to live as children, Christ is the Saviour who seeks to bring us thither, the Holy Spirit is the indwelling Friend, love is the law of life, and the holy victory may be ours.

Now what I am affirming is, that the

best explanation of the power of Christianity among men is that Christianity is true: that Christianity sets forth the things of the soul as they are. The power is best accounted for by supposing that the true representation of the meaning of the soul's life is here given, so that to experience what Christianity proposes is to experience the thing that is, and thus to find eternal foundations. If this were so, then power would follow, even the power that attends upon reality when it is put to the test. If this were so, then the power of the living God himself would go forth in Christianity, to make it effective. That this is so, I thoroughly believe. The Christian experience is experience of the eternal reality. This is why Christianity, presented in its spiritual simplicity, has always appealed successfully to the best that is in man: it is adapted to man's soul and life, and man to it. Indeed, all intelligent being is adapted to Christianity and Christianity to it, because Christianity sets forth the realities that give to all intelligent being its significance. Tertullian told in the early centuries of "the human soul which is naturally Christian;" by which he meant that between the constitution and destiny of the human soul and the religion that we have in Christ there is a natural affinity and a mutual adaptation. He was right. In Christianity the soul breathes the native air of the world for which it was born, and meets the announcement and experience of the truth for which it was made. Consequently it is the lower elements in the soul's life that draw it away from Christ, while the worthiest elements are responsive to his touch. Sound judgment may often bring strong objection against certain interpretations of the great realities, which may have been offered as if they were identical with them, but when we come to the realities themselves, behold,

they are good, and the noblest in the soul
affirms it. Christ calls for the best and
worthiest that man is capable of, and
every one that is of the truth hears his
voice. This power in Christianity to win
the response of the best in man is good
evidence that the voice is indeed the voice
of truth.

I have claimed that the truth of Christianity is the best explanation of the age-long power of Christianity. Yet in any adequate account of that power as actually at work there is one other thing to be mentioned. I must speak a word about its manner of laying hold upon men. Even truth is not always powerful. Even truth assented to, and truth believed, may sometimes fail of power. There was an element abundantly present in the life of the first Christian days, and present more or less at every stage of the long Christian movement, that must be counted in before we have placed in sight the entire material out of which power was made. We must take account of the mighty element of feeling. It is when realities are felt to be realities that they become powerful in the life of mankind.

Here we have to acknowledge a strange and almost incurable error. We very well know that in the moral and religious realm the impulse of feeling is needed if truth is to go forth to victory, and yet we are constantly overlooking it. We are constantly assuming that truth is to be influential upon men chiefly through the intellect. To the intellect, we think, truth makes its appeal. Truth can be stated. It belongs to the mind, it is to be handled in thought, it is to be estimated by the judgment. Truth can be accepted as truth, — that is, as correct, valid, and worthy to be held, — and what more is there to be done? It can doubtless be completed or enriched by further additions or modifications, brought in by the same process of the intellect continued: the statement of it can be made more satisfactory, and the uses of it more plain, but we do not habitually look to other processes than these as equally important. Anything that cannot be clearly stated, we sometimes allow ourselves to say, cannot be true, and certainly cannot be expected to exert power upon men. With this general idea about truth we make our statements as accurate as we can. We draw up our creeds and confessions, and are satisfied with our expression of truth, and declare that this, now clearly stated, is what we hold; and then we assume that the truth in the case has been adequately treated, and expect it to be powerful. In fact, we have often made up our creeds somewhat as a geologist makes up his description of the geological column, or a chemist his statement of the result of his analysis. We set forth the thing that we suppose to be correct, and are content, under the impression that truth is now ready for the wars.

And then very often we are disappointed. Truth thus equipped does not seem after all to be prepared for victorious battle. Statements do not win the day. The fact is that in the moral and religious realm thought, be it ever so clear, is only the preparation for power, not the very means of power itself. Power comes with feeling. Truth becomes effective by being felt to be truth. Stated in accurate forms it has a very neat appearance, and is convenient for reference and consultation, but there is no inward necessity that we should do anything about it. Not until some one feels that something is true does that something go out with effective power into the world. Unfelt knowledge is scarcely more fruitful than ignorance. Unfelt truth lies unused. In order to become effective, truth must be perceived as truth in the sensitive part of the interior life, whence the compelling influence upon the springs of action proceeds. If the outcome of the life of Jesus had been ever so clear and true a set of propositions, written out to be preserved, and there had been nothing more, we might never have heard of Christianity. There would have been no Christianity, but only a teaching. When the truth that Jesus imparted to his friends came to be felt as truth, and influential in the realm of the affections, then it came to have power, and only then.

But the truth that Jesus had given them did come to be felt as truth. This is exactly the thing that did happen. The reality took possession of the men, the Spirit showed it to them, and then the Christian power was born. We have in the New Testament the vivid portrayal of this very thing. I wish I might set before you the New Testament picture of the early Christian feeling. If I attempt it, you will not think that I am claiming that those first Christians did full justice to the realities of which I speak. I am not claiming that, for of course I know the imperfectness of it all, since it was all human. Yet I am not drawing a false picture, for the sense of these realities was genuine, and to represent it is to show the very thing that set Christianity in motion as a living force.

The first Christian reality to enter into the world of feeling appears to have been the Saviourhood of Jesus. It now came to pass that his disciples grasped the meaning of what they had seen and heard, and it came home to them with moving power. In the realm of feeling it now was real to them that for their sake he had lived and died and risen again, and was now triumphant in God's glory. They felt that they had a Saviour from their sin and loss, who filled them with new life which was life eternal. Christ had brought them home to God. To God? and what was God to them now, in this new day of feeling? God was not to them an article of faith in creed, but a reality in their own life. God was a reality that redeemed them from sin and fear and low living, and from mortality itself; and the power of this reality was actually upon them, to make all things new. They felt themselves at home with God, forgiven, accepted, made his children, domiciled with him in the home of the spirit. Nay, more and closer, God was not merely with them, he was in them. Their belief in the Holy Spirit was simply their sense of the inwardness of this divine gift, their feeling of God within. It was their consciousness that God had come nearer than to be among them, but had passed the door of their being and was inhabiting them as a temple or a home. And now they felt, yes, felt, that love was the atmosphere of their being. The love of God and Christ had been poured out around them and within, and love constituted their very life. So love, in the fine forms of fellowship, kindness, mutual helpfulness, and missionary zeal, became a life and power among the Christians: they actually loved one another, and felt the flame of love within themselves. And in the same manner the remaining element, the reality of a successful Christian holiness and victory, became a vital thing. Men now felt that great things were possible: they not merely thought it and affirmed it as a matter of belief, as we are always ready to do, but felt it, as we sometimes do not. Hence naturally sprang courage and high endeavor, and splendid success. Religion passed into virtue, because the possibility of high success was felt, and livingly believed in. Reality got possession of feeling, and then the day of power had come.

In form, I have now been speaking of the first days and the springing-up of power, but in fact, I have described what has given power to Christianity in all times. Where do you find your powerful men, — your Augustine, Luther, John Wesley? Where are your reformers, puritans, leaders? They are men of feeling, in whom realities live. They need not be emotional men, in the popular sense of that word, but they are men of feeling in the nobler sense, men to whom the Christian realities are living things, felt in their greatness and importance. When have been the ages of power? When, but when the sense of God and Christ came in, and thought was warmed to vigor, and faith became a passion? Who are the weaker men, and when have come the times of feebleness? The weaker men, for the aggressive purposes of God, are the men who, whatever they may think, do not feel: and the feebler periods are those in which the pulses have run low and the great realities found but dull response in the affections and emotions of the Christian people. Power goes with feeling.

All this is just as simple as I said it was. The power of Christianity resides in the twofold fact that Christianity is true, and is felt as true. There is reality, and there is sense of reality, — and then there is power. The reality that we have in Christ is worthy to be profoundly felt, and the sense of such reality as this ought to be sufficient to move the world. When it was anything like adequate, it has moved the world.

It may seem to some one that I am building too much on feeling, or the sense of something being true. Feeling, it may be objected, is no test of truth. We may feel, most intensely, something unreal: wherefore the sense of reality in the Christian testimony must not be taken as valid proof of that testimony. To this I should say that certainly feeling often takes hold on error, and becomes the stimulant of folly. Feeling is no proof of truth. But I would add that neither is feeling any evidence that truth is absent, and the presence of it does not establish a probability that truth is not there. Is not feeling the normal accompaniment of truth? Reality and the sense of reality ought to be inseparable companions. It is the perfection of relation between man and truth that man shall feel the thing that is, and be dull to the thing that is not. If there is reality present, and reality that concerns the soul, it is the normal and worthy thing for the sensitive soul, perceiving its presence, to feel with the keenest intensity the seriousness, the preciousness, the glory, of that which is so real. Certain it is that eternal and necessary realities, that touch upon the life and destiny of the soul, are worthy to stir the deepest feeling, according to their character. Hence, in spite of all objection from the fallibility of feeling, I look upon the Christian power as a noble confirmation of the truth of Christianity. The combination of facts is this. Proclamation is made of certain alleged realities. They are realities in the eternal order of things, pertaining to the character of eternal Being and the relation of man to the eternal love and holiness. The proclamation reaches the hearts of certain men, and in a sincere experience the men are possessed by the warm and living certainty that the proclamation brings them truth. They cast themselves upon the alleged realities, and find them solid, and feel them true. Now there springs up in them a life rich and sweet with holy graces. Their destiny is provided for, their duty grows real to them, their life at home with God transforms their character. The foundations of being now stand clear and strong for them. Warm and urgent love springs up strong in their hearts, and they become heralds of life and grace to other souls. The world grows sweeter and purer by reason of their presence. Hindrances to their higher life and their holy efficiency are on every side, and nothing about them attains to the ideal of perfection, and yet they continue age after age in the world, and the realities are proclaimed after two thousand years essentially as they were at first, and the same kind of power goes forth into the world from the people of the faith. What does all this mean? It means that truth is here. Each part of this great process tends to validate all the rest. The one great thing that is rendered daily more certain to us is that the alleged realities from which the process took its start are realities indeed. The structure honors the foundation. The power of Christianity, related as it is to the high character of Christianity, to its fitness to serve as key to the meaning of existence, and to its ability to bless all whom it touches, is a living evidence that the whole is true, and the foundation of Christianity is laid in the verities of God.

A word now from the practical side, about the power of Christianity as something that we all have to do with. Some of us are preaching Christianity, and glory in our work. Some, without preaching it, are trying to live it, and to commend it as they may. Some of us are listening to it from the outside, perhaps with conviction that it is true, perhaps without it. In one question we are all interested, each in his own way: I mean the question where the power of Christianity at present may reasonably be expected to reside and be discovered. What is a fair statement as to the seat of power in Christianity to-day? What shall we who wish to commend Christianity rely upon? and what shall we who listen to Christianity attune our hearts to respond to?

Perhaps for this moment it may help us to divide power into its two parts, — value and efficiency. The value of Christianity, upon which we must rely for power with men, resides in its truth, in the sense in which its truth has now been represented. The fact that in the central affirmations of Christianity the central realities of existence are affirmed, — this is the value of Christianity, and this is the seat of power. If this were not so, Christianity would be simply one of the vain imaginings of men; for it does profess to set forth the eternal verity. The eternal verity it does set forth. Christianity describes you as you are, in view of the true and abiding tests: it tells you what you need, offers you what you must have, exhibits life as it is, leads you to your right and normal place in God, shows you the right way to live your daily life, gives you the true conception of the world you live in, inspires you with the motive that is right forever, and gives you actual possession of the good concerning which the nations of mankind have now theorized and now agonized since human life began. This is the value of Christianity, and this is the truth to set forth, in various parts and forms, for the convincing and winning of men. The value of Christianity lies in its bringing the message of truth, and telling the things that are, — and, beyond this, in its having the power to conform us to things as they are, and bring us to our true home in God. And when the message has been uttered, and has sunk down into our hearts so that we can perceive of what sort it really is, we find this infinitely great, consoling and uplifting word at the centre of it, that the real is the good: the eternally real is the eternally good: eternal being is holy and gracious: our best is the finite counterpart of the infinite goodness: and hope rather than fear, confidence rather than doubt, is the keynote of existence.

This is the appeal to make. It can be made in a thousand forms, but this is the tone that should sound through all of them. This also is the appeal to listen for, and to listen to. When Christianity is presented to you in this tone and spirit, there is something there that no one can afford to miss. Let other appeals pass by you if you must, but never fail to have an ear for this great appeal of value.

If we ask where we are to look for efficiency in the present Christianity, — that is to say, what is to make it now effective in drawing men to its side and maintaining its active force, — we must say nothing that would obscure the efficiency of its value. Here first we must look for power, to the clear and enthusiastic presentation of the glorious view of the value of Christianity at which I have just hinted. It is by virtue of its truth that Christianity must win its way, and nothing must be said that will propose any substitute for this, or lead to reliance upon any other means of power as equal to this. Yet we cannot overlook the fact that the efficiency of truth among men depends in great measure upon the strength and vividness of the sense of truth in those who hold it forth. That the Christian people may have a rich and constraining sense of the truth that they are offering to the world, this is the next thing needful for the efficiency of our religion. I have read a criticism upon the converts that a visitor found in some of the mission-fields in Asia, to the effect that although they showed the signs of sincerity in their new faith, they did not have the appearance of men who were enthusiastically full of the feeling that they had in their new faith the best thing in the world and the best thing that the heart of man could imagine. The criticism was altogether a friendly one. I do not know how just it was, but from what I know of Christians in America I am prepared to believe that it was not unfair to new-born Christians in the East. It is our defect that we lack so much the sense of having the best thing in the world, and the best thing in any world, in our Christian faith. We say that we have it, and hold it as our theory, but we do not feel it with a constraining gladness and an enthusiastic zeal. The coming of such a sense of our heavenly gift is needful if we are to have the power that we desire.

We often say that our time is not favorable to enthusiasm in spiritual things; and it is largely true. We are in a day of scientific thought, and of critical activity. It is a great period of transition, in which all that can be removed is being shaken, that the things that cannot be shaken may remain. Amid so many questions as are abroad in our time, how, it is asked, can we maintain an enthusiastic confidence? Who knows what we shall next be invited to surrender, or at least to modify? How shall we keep our sense of the reality of the things that our religion tells us of? and how shall we dare invite intelligent men in such a time to cast in their lot with our religion? Must we not keep along as well as we can till a period of firmer confidence dawns upon us, hoping by and by to be able to commend our faith more strongly? And would it not be as well for our friends who have not received Christianity to wait until that better day, before accepting it as true and vital for themselves?

To this I answer, that I am profoundly convinced that our generation needs just such a conception of Christianity as I have endeavored to present in these three addresses, and such an experience as I have declared to be of the substance of our religion. We want to see the simplicity of our religion, and to hold as essential to it only what really is essential. We often

overburden ourselves for the Christian
purpose. We undertake to hold too much.
We bind our theories and interpretations
in as a part of the substance of Christianity. If a few of us alone could do this,
the way might look easier, at least to us,
but the trouble is that others who dissent
from us do the same, and Christianity becomes weighted with a variety of conflicting theories as to the meaning of its
experimental facts. If we go back to the
beginnings, we find a declaration of eternal
realities, such as each soul of man needs
to know, and can rest in, and find eternal
life by knowing. For my own part, I am
content with calling my fellow-men to
accept and live by these realities. This
I can do, and this I do, with the utmost
confidence. I believe that the God and
Father of the Lord Jesus Christ is the living God, the only God that there is, and
that led by Jesus Christ we may all come
home to him where we belong, and live our

normal life by being Christians. To the life of love in God I believe that the Holy Spirit of power is leading us. This I believe to be the right way for high and low, for ignorant and learned. This I would as soon declare in a great university as in the lowliest country meeting-house. This message I do not have to defend as I should be obliged to defend an elaborate scheme of thought. I will discuss the scheme of thought that is involved in the message, when and where it is necessary, but the Christianity that I preach I preach because it is true to the eternal realities, and is fit to be received at once by any soul that desires to live in accordance with the things that are. I am not claiming for myself a power that corresponds to this secret of power that I believe in. But I am anxious that the Christian people should learn that their Christian doctrine consists in the truth that they possess in the common Christian experience, and know that its power dwells in its reality, and in their sense of its reality. To what should we look for power if not to this, that the Christian people know what they possess, and offer it for what it is, an experimental possession of the eternal verities? The way of simplicity and confidence is the way of power.

I am thankful for the opportunity to speak these words in this presence. May the power of the Christian truth rest upon us all.

www.ingramcontent.com/pod-product-compliance
Lightning Source LLC
Chambersburg PA
CBHW030314170426
43202CB00009B/1003